FARMING DREAMS

FARMING DREAMS
Knud Sørensen

Translated from the Danish by
Michael Goldman

SPUYTEN DUYVIL
New York City

ACKNOWLEDGEMENTS:

I am grateful to the editors at the following journals for first publishing these poems:

Rattle: "The Record of Conduct Book"
Cider Press Review: "Production"
Meat for Tea: "The Dream" and "The Summer"
TAB Journal:
"When Hans Nielsen's farm was cut in half by the county road"
Drafthorse Journal: "Planting time. Months before", "Winter day with snow," "Foreclosure," and "The numbers"
Apple Valley Review: "A True Story" and "To Work, I Say"

THE DANISH ARTS FOUNDATION

© Knud Sørensen, Copenhagen
Published by agreement with Gyldendal Group Agency
Translation © 2016 Michael Goldman
ISBN 978-1-944682-64-4 hdc.

Library of Congress Cataloging-in-Publication Data

Names: Sørensen, Knud, 1928- author. | Goldman, Michael (Michael Favala), translator.
Title: The dream about farming / Knud Sørensen; translated by Michael Goldman.
Description: New York City : Spuyten Duyvil, 2016.
Identifiers: LCCN 2016020154 | ISBN 9781944682132
Subjects: LCSH: Sørensen, Knud, 1928---Translations into English. | Agriculture--Poetry. | Farm life--Poetry. | Denmark--Poetry.
Classification: LCC PT8176.29.O239 .A2 2016 | DDC 839.811/74--dc23
LC record available at https://lccn.loc.gov/2016020154

Contents

Introduction	v
Planting time. Months before	1
Winter day with snow	2
Only the middle of May	4
The summer	5
Summer drought	6
Harvest portrait	8
While we still have it	9
The Record of Conduct Book	10
Identity	12
The clouds	14
The cows	15
To work, I say	17
The slide rule	18
The red coffee pot	20
The revolution in Tøving	21
Foreclosure	22
The map has no symbol for pain	25
When Hans Nielsen's farm was cut in half by the county road	26
A true story	28
There are two ways	29
The numbers	30
Danish farm country	31
Production	33
Under the table	34
Tøving today	35
Momentary picture	40
The Unseen	41
And he knows that the others are there	43
Reflections on a few decades	45
On culture	48
On time	49
On the earth	50
The dream	52
On eternity	53

Translator's Introduction

I first encountered Knud Sørensen's poetry at the local library, when I was living in Denmark in the mid-1990s. I read every book of his they had, and eventually bought his *Selected Poems* before I moved back to the US. Nearly 20 years later, when I started to translate Danish poetry, I knew that I wanted to translate his work. I think his poetry made such a long-standing impression on me because it deftly revisited an era of cultural pride and tragedy that I had not encountered before in literature: the era of the disappearance of family farms.

The town where I grew up in Southern New Jersey had 82 farms in 1930. Today there is one farm left. In the US during the twentieth century, nearly 30 million people left farming. There are lots of reasons for this—technology, economics, politics. But what statistics and trends don't show is the broken link of families' and communities' cultural heritage as people left the farms. Certainly practical knowledge has been lost, but also lost has been the spirit of the interdependent farming community and the sense of personal identity that often results from a lifelong commitment to a piece of land and a community. This exodus from agriculture has been repeated throughout the world. In Denmark, where nearly every square meter of the country is arable soil, the exodus from the farmland created a national cultural shift. The final generation of farmers in countless families had to leave their land, and in their place, bedroom communities emerged and agribusiness grew. Sørensen is quick to point out that these farmers were largely successful in their new lives. They had steadfast constitutions that were welcomed in urban workplaces. Yet still the ghosts remain: the ghosts of ancestors, the ghosts of a sense of connection to the earth, or a connection to a community—all these "unquantifiables" that somehow still reside in many of us, regardless of the geography of our family origins.

The numbers do not tell the whole story. And it is not altogether a happy tale. I sense that, because of the tragic emotions connected to this era, we, as a population, have largely suppressed our sense of loss. In contrast to the farming culture, today it is the technological—the futuristic and slick—that is peddled to us as the ideal of human achievement. Still we may feel something lacking, like a sense of place or an ancestral heritage. Herein lies the challenge of a great writer, to reunite us with our story of loss, and help us to appreciate the pride and connection even as we feel the tragedy. This is what Knud Sørensen achieves above all else. In his poetry we are reminded of the glory and of the heartache in "Farming Dreams."

Michael Favala Goldman
Florence, Mass. USA
January, 2015

Message from Knud Sørensen

Som lyriker kan man komme ud for en perlerække af gode oplevelser. Det kan begynde med, at nogle ord, f.eks. udspringende af et synsindtryk, begynder at rumstere et sted i ens hoved, og de ord finder så sammen i digtform. Så ser man, at det digt passer fint ind i den sammenhæng, man i øjeblikket er optaget af. Fremkomsten af digtet i bogform er så som oftest sidste led i rækken. Men så kan det lykkelige også ske, at man en dag ser digtet omsat kongenialt til et andet sprog, og det, der før var en perlerække lukker sig om sig selv til en perlekæde. Det er fuldbragt.

Knud Sørensen
Mors, Denmark
Jan 2015

Translation

As a poet I am often exposed to pleasant experiences as if they were an array of pearls. It might start with a few words springing from a visual impression, for example. Then the words rummage around someplace inside my mind, eventually joining together into the form of a poem. Then I see that the poem fits nicely into the theme that I just happen to be currently occupied with. Appearance of the poem in book form is usually the last pearl on the string. But then an additional delight may occur—that one day the poem gets translated suitably into another language, and what before was a string of pearls becomes a necklace. It is complete.

Planting time. Months before.

Windrows of threshed hay lie
where the combine drove.
He starts running
with a burning clump on a pitchfork,
he ignites the field, running
back and forth he tosses the fire
from row to row and the flames
thunder across the field, the sun
blurs hanging quivering
in the sky and ash and dust
drift over the ground, his face
turns black and streaked with sweat splashing
down over his cheeks, he runs
the flames jump, he shouts at the fire
he jeers and rages, and the air
fills with smoke, it gets dark, dark. He runs
across the field, lungs burning, following the flames,
dripping with sweat and covered with ash and dust,
he breathes in gasps, arms and legs painful appendages
he keeps going, keeps going, heavily, but keeps going,
the flames die and he stops, walks
slowly towards home trailing
the stench of burnt land behind him.

He sits one day on a tractor
and plows the scorched field.
Then goes and waits
through the winter
for planting time.

Winter day with snow

Already before daybreak
he notices that the ground
is white. A weaker darkness
behind the bedroom curtains
and he turns on the light
and gets up
and pulls back the curtain
and the farmyard
is more visible than usual
and the light
reflected more strongly
than before, and he
gets dressed
and walks across the soft farmyard
to the morning milking
to the feeding
and the mucking out.
When he re-emerges
to the farmyard
the sun is up
and it's shining
and the sky is blue and the land
is still white, the frost
has hollowed out the air
so you think you can breathe in all space
without getting filled, and everything
is still white
the farmyard, the roofs, the garden
and the fields that almost disappear
and suddenly he knows
what he has to do
on a day like this.
After coffee
he drives the tractor out

gets the liquid manure tank
primes the pump
so its sound becomes full
and inescapable
and all day long he drives
across the fields
coloring them brown again.
It's good to have livestock
it's good to have a thousand gallons of liquid manure
on a day like this
good to fill
this frozen void
with a heavy and fertile smell.
He smiles
now they are cursing him
in all the cars up there on the road.

Only the Middle of May

He stands
and looks
out over his field.
The grain is green
just as grain should be
in May, it's dense
like grain also should be
in May, and he lets his fingers
glide through it
and he looks more and more thoughtful.
It's the middle of May and already
so high. It was how it got warm
so suddenly
he says, it was the rain that came
at too perfect a time
he says, it shouldn't have been
this far along
and he pulls up a couple of stems
and he looks at them
and he bends them
and he snaps them in half
and he crumples them up
and throws them down. I should
have saved the fertilizer
he says, this grain has had
it too easy.

THE SUMMER

The landscape of summer
shall be populated
with cows: waddling
pedestrians, four-legged
marvels, motivated
by insatiability and an ever-
wakeful curiosity.
Summer days
shall be filled
with productive laziness
with instinctive heavy cud-
chewing. Summer sounds
shall be the dull thuds
of ruminated nature
and summer's joy
the broad meaty backs
that one's hand likes
to give gentle pats
one quiet evening while the dew
starts to settle.

Summer drought

The barometer won't do
what he wants.
He taps on it
but the high pressure
is unmoving.
Every morning
this stubborn pointer
every day
this sun much too near
turning the grass
to brownish dust
burning the tips
of the grain
turning the sugar beets
into small wrinkled knots
and every day
is even longer
than the one before
even though the calendar
says differently.
He lies awake at night
thinking about clouds
he lies awake at night
in order to hear a sound
of drops falling
but hears only
the dried-out wood frame creaking
he lies awake at night
holding onto the dark
to conjure wind, clouds, rain
he lies awake in the dark
until the first ray of sun
draws a silhouette
of stiff leaves

on the yellow curtain.
Then he lies there for a couple more hours
and tries not to wake.
Later
he has to get moving.
He walks with difficulty
it tenses his whole body
to see country like this.

Harvest Portrait: The day before

He goes out and looks at the grain
the barley has bowed its head
tomorrow, yeah
tomorrow.
He takes a rake
and does the rose bed
one more time
he goes out and looks at the grain
the barley has bowed its head
tomorrow, yeah
tomorrow.
He takes a broom
and sweeps out the barn
one more time
he goes out and looks at the grain
the barley has bowed its head
tomorrow, yeah
tomorrow.
He goes in and slowly dials
the telephone. He gets some oil
and greases the machines
one more time
he goes out and looks at the grain
tomorrow, yeah
tomorrow.
He prunes the hedge and mows the grass
but probably doesn't have time to paint
the flagpole.
tomorrow, yeah
tomorrow.
The barley has bowed its head.

While we still have it

He can stand there like that and be happy
for the grass-covered ground
for the grain, the sugar beets, the seed crops,
he can stand there and be happy
for the earth softened by frost in the winter
made ready for cultivation
he can stand there like that and be happy
for the spring's warm rain, for the sun
for green and yellow color as far
as the eye can see, he can
stand there like that and be happy
for the earth that goes belly up
towards October, he can
stand there like that and dream
hour after hour
he can stand there like that
and think about himself.

The Record of Conduct book

Danish domestic workers were required to maintain these books from 1832 to 1921. Issued at confirmation, the book held record of employment, conduct, and wages for the individual.

Every first of November
she took out her Record of Conduct book
and laid it on the table in front of the man
on the farm that she now would be leaving
and the man got out a pen and ink
and tried the pen on his fingertip
or on the corner of a piece of scrap paper
and then he remembers his glasses
and gets them and sets himself down
and writes slowly and carefully
and with the proper pressure on the downstrokes:
The girl Karen Jensdatter has served me
loyally and with good conduct from the first of November last year
to this date, and he
dates and signs and she
curtsies and says thank you, thank you for everything
and she walks out the door and she still holds open
the Record of Conduct book so the ink
has time to dry, and she thinks
that now begins a new year in a yet unknown place
with a yet unknown master and mistress and maybe
with some yet unknown luck, and sometimes she also
has to go to the churchwarden to report her move
from one parish to another
and every first of November she hopes
that it will be her last first of November of this kind
and the years pass and all the young farmhands that have property
get married and the years pass and not until she is
38 does Kresten inherit
his parents house with no land and she gets

her last entry in the book and her real life
begins,
as a sharecropper's wife, mother
to a pair of girls that quickly
are too young for her
and full of insecurity
and go out into the world with new
authorized Record of Conduct books in their hands.

Identity

It was the abundance of children
that you noticed.
And the house. That such a house
could contain
so many children,
barefoot, clogged
boys, girls
but always
nameless, considered
only as a species
of the region's farmers
only as
one of Lars Peder's girls
or as
one of Lars Peder's boys
and as a species
they spread themselves across the region
planted
in the farmhands' and maidservants' rooms
later
exiled to the city
to the capital
to America or
to an all too early grave
in a corner of the cemetery,
a single one
remained in the area however
grew up to an increasingly meager
and sinewy life, from boy
to farmhand, from farmhand
to day-laborer, husband, farmworker,
populated a couple of rented rooms
in an old pensionary house
with a new generation of children

and received — almost — a name through them:
Lars Peders Kresten's boys
Lars Peders Kresten's girls
until
the Small Landholder Movement
and the Parcel Development Association
made him into Small Landholder Kresten Larsen
and gave him a registry number
so his sun at long last
got a piece of land on which to shine.

The Clouds

The clouds have no home —
restlessly they drift across the sky
with no goal other than the moving
away, away.
They don't worry about the shapes
first a dog
then a face with a warty nose
and then again just a cloud
in continual change
from image to image.
They never learn about the seriousness
before being dissolved in space
or falling to the earth
as the saddest
and most useful
of all things.

The Cows

If it weren't for the cows
—the black and white Holsteins, the red Holsteins
and the small plain Jerseys —
if it weren't for the cows,
we would not have
a green Denmark.
We would have grain, of course,
it's true color is gold,
and grain is something second-rate,
that is only eaten
by pigs and humans, no
if it weren't for the cows,
if these mounds of meat
did not wade around in grass to their knees
always grouped tightly together, always
— almost —
in step, if it weren't for the cows
we would not have Denmark
like a green dream about eternity.

But the dream
is in constant danger:
There is always one cow
that is different, one cow
that keeps from the flock, one cow
that turns its head the other way, one cow
that eats, while the others are chewing their cud, one cow
who nears the visitor
with its tongue out, prepared
to show a coarse approachability and seeking
beyond itself, there is always one cow
standing licking and sniffing
and looking far off past the fence
and wishing

for a life as a not-cow, maybe
as a hen in a cage
or a pig on the third floor
or a human on the fourteenth, there it stands
uneasy, unsure, unaware
of its own heaviness, there it stands
holding one end of a lengthy
wistful moo,
when the stranger leaves.

The real cows
lie in the grass.
They chew their cud
as cows always
have chewed their cud.
They only look within,
and they are green all the way to their souls.
The real cows
are reincarnated farmers —
it is for them
that the grass grows,
the sun shines
and the rain falls.
It is for them that the seasons change,
so the world is always
invariably new —
it is for the real cows
who are reincarnated farmers
— and for the real farmers
who are reincarnated cows.

To Work, I Say

So I grab
the spade handle.
It is smooth
from hands taking hold
colored
by the sweat of hands
and I stick the spade in the earth
and step on it.
It glides down
with a nice dry sound
and I tilt the handle back
and lift and turn. The earth
is black and crumbly.
I stick the spade in the earth
and step on it. The earth
is black and crumbly the smell
is raw almost moldy. I
stick the spade in the earth
and step on it, expose
worms, pebbles and half-rotten
stalks. I stick the spade
in the earth and step on it.
Square yard
after square yard becomes loose
black and crumbly
and a tiredness
creeps through the spade
into my body.
To work
I say
is to release the earth
from tiredness.

The Slide Rule. A Preface

The slide rule
was not just a tool
for calculation
but was in its approached
exactness
a challenge to the engineer's
healthy and human
doubt.
Every answer
was met with the question:
"Does this
seem probable —
Is this
in accord
with common sense and experience?"
as sometimes
the healthy doubt over
a comma's placement
comes into question:
"Is this result
a desired
result?"

When the slide rule
was replaced by
electronics
the approached
was replaced
by the doubtless
the careful judgment
replaced with excitement
over the enormous possibilities,
when the slide rule
was replaced by buttons

the critical attitude
became automatic acceptance,
first of the number
then of the technically possible
as an expression of a political
goal.

It is doubt
I am seeking
with this eulogy
of the slide rule,
it is doubt
I wish to see built into
every cycle,
it is the human sense
I desire in order to be able
to place each comma.
It is the future
I am thinking of.

The Red Coffee Pot. A Summer Morning

Just this
this coffee pot is red
just this

on a blue tablecloth
—cool with yellow butter
crumbs
soft knives
and orange marmalade

a smile
and teeth like milk-white bone splinters
in an anonymous neck
the newspaper over a chair back
just this

to write words without fever
just this
that this coffee pot is red
the end.

The Revolution in Tøving

In the middle of the afternoon
we go in for coffee and I
am the least familiar one so I sit
at the one long side and the two neighbors
who today are buyer and seller sit
at each end and the wife
walks back and forth with her cup in
hand but sits down now and then
on the edge of a chair. I let

the sugar go by but say
that I would like some cream and the wife says
that unfortunately she only has milk and the husband says
that their cow is a bit slow. I say
that's no problem I use milk
at home anyway and I use it just
to cool it down. So

we eat rolls and coffee cake and cookies
and chat about different things and about the difficulties
of farming and the wife says
that it's not so strange that no one
stays on the land anymore and
the two table-end-men don't say anything
because of course everything is already settled. I say
The times have changed.

So quickly we switch to talking about the times
and the other times. About back when
the county road got paved. About the first
electric fence. The first tractor. All this
we talk about in the spring of '71.
It is a cosy afternoon in the country.

FORECLOSURE
(Ole Andersen disappears)

Ole Andersen
sits in his kitchen.
It is a quiet noontime, the sounds
are the clock's movement, the hum of the refrigerator,
and the drip of the hot water faucet. Ole Andersen
is listening for another sound
from the sunshine
from the newly fallen snow
that clearly shows
that he has been in the barn twice
this morning. Now he listens, now
he just sits and listens.

The sound arrives. The sound is driving on four wheels
into the farmyard, turns,
stops in front of the door
and out steps the lawyer
and out steps the sheriff
with the foreclosure book in his hand
and Ole Andersen rises
and goes through his kitchen
through his utility room, out his door
and is no longer Ole Andersen
but defaulter.

Defaulter greets them quietly. Defaulter
hears the ball-point pen drown out the sheriff's voice
when it is entered in the record book
that the sheriff delivered papers on
the 19th of January 1981 at 1:45pm
and executed
petition from the Danish Farmers Credit Union
regarding bankruptcy auction of the property

reg. nr. 42b Tøving City, Galtrup
— foreclosure.
We have to take a look around, says the sheriff.
The door to the machine shed is open.

1 tractor, make Volvo, year 1974, red
sheriff makes a note of it
1 tractor, make Ferguson, year 1956
sheriff makes a note of it
1 baler, make Ferguson, nearly new
sheriff makes a note of it
1 double plow, make Skjold
sheriff makes a note of it and lets his gaze fall on
various hand tools, a single rubber boot
a wreck of a work wagon, a can of oil
and the lawyer shakes his head and the sheriff
shakes his head. Then
they walk over to the livestock building.

1 sow with 8 piglets, says the lawyer
and the sheriff makes a note of it
1 sow with 10 piglets, says the lawyer
and the sheriff makes a note of it
1 sow with 8 piglets, says the lawyer
9, says defaulter, they count
one sow with 9 piglets, says the lawyer
and the sheriff makes a note of it
1 sow with ear tag no. 213
1 sow
2 market hogs
6 feeder pigs, says the lawyer
and the sheriff makes a note of it:
Nothing encumbered with lien.
Thus it is carried out.
Foreclosure completed.

They go out into the yard. That was that,
says the sheriff. Won't you have
a cup of coffee? asks defaulter
trying to regain his lost
identity, my wife isn't around
but won't you have a cup of coffee?
and the sheriff smiles and shakes his head
and says that they're busy, you know they have
other cases waiting, and he nods goodbye
and the lawyer nods goodbye
and they get in their car
and start it up and drive away.
Defaulter stands and watches them go.
Then he goes inside.
Defaulter sits down
at the kitchen table that Ole Andersen
left behind.

THE MAP HAS NO SYMBOL FOR PAIN

On the map it looks easy:
a line slightly changed,
a line that leads where before
there was no line, a line
that is erased and disappears
into history. On the map
it looks so easy
so easy
to change the world, so painless
—for the map has no symbol
for pain.

On the map it is so easy.
The lines don't protest, the surfaces
adapt themselves like it is their nature
to adapt themselves,
the buildings disappear without help of bulldozers
and are replaced perhaps in the next second
by a different configuration, that's how easy
it is to change the society
this way. No one protests
since each conversation
occurs in the map's language, and the map's language
doesn't contain words like hope and pain
but only has averting words
like *necessity* and *structure accommodation*.
It is so easy to safeguard
one's professional innocence
in that language.

Not until the day
that the map shall be attested as true
does one's hand begin to tremble
and one's signature
becomes more and more illegible.

When Hans Nielsen's farm was cut in half by the county road

The property lies in slightly undulating terrain approx. 30 ac. on a uniform lot favorable for agriculture. The buildings sit along the town road in the northeast corner. (Farmhouse modernized in '58. New pighouse in '64). At the appraisal in '69 the property was assessed as following: Improvements 126,000, land 49,000. The family consists of a man and wife and a daughter living at home (office intern).

It starts with baseless rumors. Then comes the notice about the survey. Then come the markers. Then comes the certified letter with summons to an inspection of the property. Then comes the day.

A couple of carfuls of county board members and technicians arrive at 10 am and take in the field conditions . The fall plowing has been done and it is not good for walking, so observations are made from the stone boundary wall. Afterwards they continue with negotiations around the table in the living room.

Presented:
As passed by the county board and approved by the cabinet minister consisting of plats, elevations, cross-sections and land register maps. Plus: Registry of owned property and copy of the summons with postal receipts. And not mentioned in the minutes: cigars, cheroots, cigarettes.

The project is reviewed. Vehicular crossings of the new road will not be constructed. Instead the establishment of smaller underpasses are suggested and detailed drawings are presented to the county board members and to Hans Nielsen. Hans Nielsen says My harrow won't fit through that. The technicians think that it can and two men go out to measure the harrow. Nielsen is right. And what if I get a combine. The 1.8 mile alternate route that would otherwise have to be used is studied.

Hans Nielsen goes out to the kitchen to talk with his wife. A county board member remarks that it's just a matter of time before the property would cease operations. Looking around the living room, the furniture is quite new. There is a 19" television and a tape-player. Hanging on the wall are a colorized aerial photograph of the farm buildings and portraits of family members at different ages. Also an agricultural board certificate that Hans Nielsen and his wife received in '58. A fly buzzes in the window sill. The air is blue from cigar smoke. Hans Nielsen comes back and says How about taking the whole thing.

It is dictated to the minutes that the lot owner desired the cut-off land area expropriated (approx. 10.4 ac.). The minutes are signed. (Compensation is referred to Assessment).

There is some chat for a few minutes about commonplace things. Like raising pigs and such. Then the visitors say goodbye. And continue on. It's 11am.

A True Story

Søren Andersen had a small farming
proprerty. Søren Andersen was old. Søren Andersen
was tired. Søren Andersen sold it to Hans Østergaard
for 81,000. Hans Østergaard bought some abutting land for 8,000 and
figured everything was pretty good. His livestock
was some of the best. Mr. B. arrived in his Volvo

and offered him 125,000 for the land and buildings and Hans
Østergaard saw the heavens open. He kept a straight face
and sold it and Mr. B. returned to Copenhagen.
And waited.

4 years later Mr. B. sold it to Mr.C. for 500,000. And
Mr. C sat down to wait. 8 months he waited. Then
he sold it to Mr. E. for 1.1 million. Insane
said people in the area. Mr. E. did not wait. He
subdivided. People bought. Profit:
700,000. Net.

In the same period the monthly social pension increased
from 682 to 1259 crowns and many hundreds of new laws
were adopted in the parliament. Søren Andersen
is still alive. He lives in "The Old Folks Home" about 1/3 of a
mile from "the place." He doesn't say much
and he doesn't like his new teeth so he doesn't
smile much either. At the election in '73
he voted like he always had done.
Everybody says
that he never had it as good
as he does now.

There Are Two Ways

to resolve a difficult situation.

Either:
You figure that it won't be profitable
to expand and modernize the barn.
You sell the livestock
and are now a farmer without cattle.
You take on some
side jobs.
It doesn't go so well.
You take on some more work and hire
a contractor to do
the farming.
It still doesn't go so well.
The work doesn't pay enough.
The contractor charges too much.
You sell the land
and find a job in an industry.
It works out.

Or:
You figure that you're history
if you don't expand and modernize.
You expand and modernize.
You apply for a state loan, a credit union loan
and a savings bank loan.
You plague your creditors.
You hope for increasing stock prices
but the day that the credit union loan comes due
the loss is huge.
You make the first payment.
You make the second payment
and a couple of harvest liens
makes the third.
Then it all becomes clear.
You sell the farm.
You find a job in an industry.
It works out.

The Numbers

In 1942 there were 456,000 full time workers in Danish farming. In 1975 the number had fallen to 161,000. In the same timeframe the number of work horses decreased from 583,000 to 13,000, and the number of tractors increased by 183,000. Therefore: 183,000 tractors made—together with other machinery, changes in production, etc. — 295,000 people and 570,000 horses superfluous.

The relationship between people and horses is natural. One person for every 2 horses. A team.

If we imagine now these superfluous 295,000 people with their superfluous horses on their way out of Danish farming, for example, across the Danish-German border by Kruså, then you have to imagine an almost infinite line of people and horses, down through Holstein, past Hamburg, on the interstate past Frankfurt, past Basel, over St. Gotthard, they reach Milan, continue, continue, and at the moment that the first person turns into St. Peter's Square in Rome, the last person leaves the border crossing at Kruså.

An exodus like this represents the exodus from Danish farming.

Danish Farm Country

In '68 when Klaus Mikkelsen
sold the farm
he was the area's last active farmer
to give up.

The new owners
ran water lines and installed
a tub and toilet.
They turned the pig house into a guest suite
and the barn into a workshop.
They had the manure pit emptied and disinfected
and made into a patio.

The yard was expanded
a little. Just like the neighbor did
and the neighbor's neighbor
and the neighbor's neighbor's neighbor
etc.

At a distance:
Danish Farm Country
with rounded hills and hedges
and green fields (or yellow
or white or black — depending
on the season)
and spread apart in the terrain
the well-maintained homesteads like monuments
to a suitable
succession.

But if it doesn't happen to
be Sunday
the monuments are deserted
and anyone can also see
that the land is leased
and neglected regarding lime
and fertilizer.

Production

There's not just barley
growing in the new Danish landscape
loneliness grows there too
and denser with each year that passes,
the combines
harvest more loneliness
than grain
and loneliness is what
slips through the milking system's tubes
with a distant and quiet rush.

Loneliness
can't be sold,
it piles up
in the steadily growing
barns and stables,
it permeates the farmyard
and the farmhouse,
it sits
in front of the television in the evening
drinking
a single cup of coffee.

He says:
I have chosen
freedom
and the right
to decide for myself.

Under the Table

It's not enough
that you've worked on the local farms
from five in the morning till seven at night
for many years.
It's not enough
that you've gone to farming school
and know everything about liquid ammonia
about managing livestock and tractor maintenance.
It's not enough.
You also need money.

And it's not enough either
that you've saved and saved
and that your tax return year after year
shows minimal expenses
and a steadily increasing bank account.
It's not enough,
because when you sit in the living room of the seller
and you've talked your way through countless cups of coffee
to something that resembles agreement
about the price on the property, the prices of small items
and about the date of change in ownership
and when you have reached that point
where only a handshake separates you from the property
the seller says, "And of course I'll want 50,000 of it
under the table." and you stiffen and your hand stops
in the middle of the movement and you don't understand
what's happening. Because no one has taught you
that money in the bank isn't money. No one
has taught you that money on your tax return
isn't money. In farming school they didn't say
that real money is off the books, and you shake your head
and you leave with your education
and your bank records and the seller picks up the telephone
and calls the next one. That's just the way it is.

Tøving Today

1.

Every year has some mornings like this:
The shadows are white and the ground
is black in the sun. Every year
has some mornings like this:
Motionless blue sky and sun
that cannot be heard. Every year
has a morning like this, you don't speak out loud,
you breathe deep, deep
all the way down into your toes you breathe and you float
away over the landscape in slow motion
like you have learned to do from movies and TV. Every year

has this kind of morning when it is right
that nothing happens, that no one
launches into their daily work, no one
drives 60 down the narrow town road, no
children go running to school, no one
has an errand at the machine shop, it is really
altogether that kind of morning
and it gets to be late morning, noon, afternoon.
And it's not right any more.

2.

What I mean is
there are plenty of sounds
but that's the seagulls.
Here far from the coast
they walk around on their webbed feet
too white, too screeching
too foreign here
where only consumers of grain should walk around
and stick their beaks in the ground. Here they fill
the fields, the air, here they sit
on the meetinghouse roof, here they sit
as if they were at home, and the meetinghouse
is used only as a platform
for seagulls. The combines
don't do gymnastics in the evening
and the milking machines don't dance the polka
in the evening, and the meetinghouse
deteriorates, the walls crumble, the windows
break, the door hangs crooked
but it's still called "Godthaab"[1]
and it still has a Board of Directors
who every year discuss: Shall we sell it
or tear it down? and the seagulls sit year after year
on the roof ridge in the middle of the blue sky
and screech out over the landscape.
Tøving today.

---

[1] Good Hope

3.

From the roof of the meetinghouse
you can't see the seagulls
sitting on the roof of the school.
Tøving School, built in 1954,
closed in 1975, since also in Tøving
the tractors don't bear children who go to school
nor has Tøving avoided the planning
that from one day to the next turns investments
into bad investments, that makes the entirety so big
that it can't be contained in the entirety, that replaces
schools with busses and replaces voices
with the sound of machines, or more accurately
that replaces voices with a dream of
machines, because the school remains dreaming
with its emptiness behind the well-maintained masonry
and the unwashed windows, dreaming about a factory,
about a workplace, about a buzzing activity
or maybe just a hobby ceramics artist
on vacation. The school dreams and the gulls sit
sleeping on the roof ridge and a car drives by
the somewhat beat-up triangular sign
that proclaims internationally to the stranger
that here, here there is a school. Drive slow
stranger, here there is a school. And the stranger
slows down and drives through the phantom:
Rural-Denmark. Present-day Tøving.

4.

He drives on and there are plenty of possibilities.
Unfathomable amounts of asphalt were poured out on the ground
when no one could nourish themselves by it any more.
The roads are laid at intervals of a few hundred yards
and between them field boundaries, stone walls and windbreaks
disappear, and Tøving becomes large uniform surfaces
two or three times a year populated by a tractor
with accompanying personnel. Tøving
becomes an idyll without distracting details. Tøving
becomes a picture of peace and relaxation.
But a picture. The stranger drives past.
Sees no people. Sees some houses
and from a single chimney rises
pensioned smoke up towards the blue sky.
The stranger sees it suddenly. The smoke, the sky.
It warms his heart and he starts dreaming
of a vacation home in this spot. But by then he's already out
of Tøving.

5.

And then it's evening. Now
there's activity in Tøving. Someone
is coming home. The foundry worker
comes home from the foundry, the bricklayer's assistant
comes home from the building site, the tanker truck driver
has left his truck and arrives home
in his Volkswagen. The nurse comes home
from the hospital, and the bank intern come home
from the bank, they arrive, everyone comes
through the deepening darkness, from the furniture factory,
from the city's stores, from the city's offices, now
they arrive home to the quiet farmyards
to the empty barns and outbuildings, now they go inside
the empty farmhouses, they turn on the lights, they prepare food,
they eat, they wash up, and for the person driving
through Tøving at night everything is how it should be.
There is light at the gables. There is light in the rooms.
Through the windows you see people at coffee tables,
at card games or in front of the television. You see
a child doing homework, a back stooped over a loom,
a newspaper floating between two hands, now finally
now finally everything is as you expected it to be. At night
people live in Tøving.

Momentary picture

Stops
during a movement
during a sensation
stops in the middle of a word
the picture freezes
everything is meaningful

The sounds are dammed up
the earth is a scream under the asphalt
behind the walls
the houses are packed with pent-up shouts
quiet
the throat is tense

and in an explosion
actions are upon us again
no one can escape
no one can reside in a picture

The Unseen

One sits in his apartment on the 5th floor
in an opaque building
and there are only opaque buildings to see
out the window
and one sits in her kitchen in the 3rd building cluster
and from the window
there are brick walls and windows to see
and one sits in his single-family home with shades rolled down
and almost doesn't dare turn the calendar page
because then the payment's due and it's his, his, his
and because the stock and bond prices
spell out a language that is devoid
of human touch
and because the payment balance dictates
what one may go and think about
they sit in their living rooms, in their kitchens
and in their houses and don't know
what they will do today
or tomorrow to make the time go by.
And one still has the memory of a movement
in the right hand
and one still has a symbol language
stored in her brain
and one still has a proficiency and a command
that no one has any use for
and they don't know one another
they don't see one another
singly
they arrive at the unemployment office
and get their stamp
and in order for charter flights to multiply
and in order for 50 Danish families every week
to buy residences in the Mediterranean
and in order for the cash registers

to set new records every day
they are placed out of sight
so no one shall see the familiar lines
from the thirties' news photographs
and get the wrong impression
and they sit in their living rooms
in their kitchens and in their single-family homes
and people is something they see on TV
and handshakes are something they exchange with doorknobs
and hunger is something that exists in Namibia
and increased mortality something that is only found in India
and other hardships are only outside the country's borders
and we all know
that the Danish gross national product
is one of the happiest
in the world.

And He Knows That the Others Are There

And he knows that the others are there
some place in the noise they are standing
with their stiff backs
with their lumbar aches
that come from the same movement
repeated, repeated year
after year. And he knows
that the others are there, some place in the noise
behind protective screens, behind masks
some place in the noise they are there
and the production numbers are increasing
and waste-product numbers
are increasing. The stiff backs, for example,
the lumbar soreness, for example,
and his injured hand. For example.
And every morning
he arrives
with his hand in a bandage
and makes his rounds of the workplace.
Let's get going
he says to the others
Don't just stand there yapping
he says and smiles
and the others smile
and for a brief second he's one
of them again
and then
he goes home to the empty house
to the radio and the newspaper from yesterday
and he sits at the table for a while
and he walks back and forth
and he lies on the sofa for a while, and not until
he sees his buddies
drive by out on the road

can he relax.
Now we're home
he thinks, now we're all home
he thinks, now we're all going to hang around
and enjoy ourselves before dinner.
God-damned work
he thinks, god-damned work
he mutters, and grabs his back
with the good hand. God-damned work.

Reflection on a Few Decades

One day Denmark sprouted up in heather.
Grain had long ago been abandoned,
sugar beets abandoned, and the coincidental growth of grass
suffocated by reindeer moss and crowberry,
by cowberry and bearberry,
and the heather advanced
towards the empty livestock buildings
with the rusted-out automatic feeding machines,
the heather advanced
towards the empty windowless farmhouses
where the wallpaper hung in damp waves
on the walls, the heather advanced
towards the collapsed barns
and made the decay romantic and picturesque,
the heather advanced, and around in it wandered
— once in a while — nature lovers and conservation people
who enjoyed the complete absence
of productive activity,
and around the universities
sat quiet students of history and economy
writing papers
about the Danish interest rate's influence
on an advantageous outcome of the battle
against surplus productivity in EU,
and the tourist associations introduced
"International Park North"
and German and Dutch farmers
took trips to European nature
and took out berry-picking licenses and went home with
crowberries and cowberries for their freezers
at their well-run farms down south.

And the heather advanced,
tangled itself together around the cities,
crept through the hedges, crawled
over the single-family homes
and made them into gypsy caves,
broke up the asphalt and sucked
the last nourishment out of the road sub-surfaces,
advanced on stores and offices, found
cracks in the facades of concrete buildings
—and the effect was like thousands of tons
of slow TNT— the heather
broke into the IT facility's programs, the heather
broke open safes, decomposed securities, erased
the portraits on coins, the heather
yes it is hard to believe , the heather
brought Denmark to a halt.

And one day
the heather grew into forest. Neglected and untended
the heather grew into forest, at first
you saw a saw-toothed horizon
and year after year
the horizon came closer, the countryside
became more green, a wilder
country, and the sounds changed, the animals
changed, and people had memories
that they didn't know the origins of,
and there were some
who left the piles of ruin
and disappeared
out into wild Denmark
and more followed
without really meaning to,
and ax blows beat
a new rhythm inside their bodies

and delicate white columns of smoke
rose towards a blue spring sky
like a new joy
flowing from the earth.
One day everyone knew
that the impossible had happened.

On Culture

And an old woman
is making her way slowly
down the sidewalk
with a cane in her right
and a shopping bag in the other
hand,
and as

she is about to cross the street
it starts to rain,
and she thinks about the grain
that she always goes to tie up
right about now,
and of course it would be best for it not to rain,
lord,
remember now,
we would like to have a couple of weeks
without rain,
and she looks around,
but it is so far to the sky,
and to the fields
and the houses are in the way
and again she feels
the rain.

Stay here,
she says
and is almost
too quiet to be heard,
stay here, rain,
and let me
receive you.

And she continues on
happily oppressed
by her fate.

On Time

It is not the wind
which beats the color
out of the grass,
it is not the wind
that gets the fruit
to fall from the farthest branches
at this moment,
and it is not the wind
that makes the clouds seek
the closest horizon No

it's no use
choosing the wind
as an explanation,
I know very well,
that it's not that
which presides out here,
but that it is time,
my one and only time,
running faster
and faster
and still running
farther away, I know very well,
that it is that
which has leapt out of my pulse
and now
— suddenly —
exults,

finally free.

On the earth

There he stands
in the midst of his world,
meaning
in the midst of his grain
but also
in the midst of that pitiful
and yellowed spot,
that probably
has gotten too much
of something chemical,
or has been hit
by a coincidental fall-out
or by an errant gene
that should have been
somewhere completely different,
and he just stands there,
and it looks increasingly
as if he were full of admiration,
rather than standing
in the midst of an identity crisis.

Then he says,
Don't think
that you can subdue
the earth.
The earth is strong
and unconquerable,
it is only
the income-producing earth
that is fragile,
he says,
it is only
the random life's earth
that can be threatened,

when the random life
scratches it
too coarsely.

Just look, he says,
when you think you have got it,
it turns it's back
in order to live a completely different life.
It has enough of them.
I only have one,
he says and almost can't
hide his laughter.
He kicks one of the clods.
Damned earth.

The Dream

I want to make it simple
and easy to understand:
You start by preparing your land and afterwards you
sow. Then the sun shines and it rains and the sun shines again
and one day the green shoots come up. So you watch
the shoots grow into plants and the plants grow and
flower and set seed and the sun shines and the seed matures
and it's time to harvest.

So you harvest. So you thresh and some of the seed you save
for sowing next spring and some of the seed you save
to use during the winter and the rest of the seed
you sell.

Over the winter you take care of your livestock.

In this way you live until you die. Everything else is just ripples
on the surface. Dairy consolidations factories revolutions sales
percentages meat cattle versus milk cows all that is unreal.
What is real is earth sun rain and the air
that is warmer in the summer than in the winter.

So simple.

On Eternity

A kestrel is suspended up there
maybe only
seconds before the dive,
and the wind sweeps across the hill,
and the grass yields,
the same way it always has,
and the earth
has that smell
that some would call
a smell of rot
others
a smell of fertility.

Someplace nearby
there is an open window
and a radio is on
in the living room inside,
and that audible tone
is the words
that flee the house
hiding themselves
like a harmony
in the wind.
The kestrel
is still suspended up there in the blue sky
and I am still standing in the grass
on a hillside
in the middle of my Danish outpost.

The sun is also
gentle and silent.

Danish author, **Knud Sørensen**, born in 1928, was a certified land surveyor for 28 years, during which he became intimate with the Danish agricultural landscape. A book reviewer for 14 years, he has also written 48 books and won over 20 literary awards. including a lifelong grant from the Danish Arts Council. In November 2014 he received the Great Prize of the Danish Academy, the highest literary award given in Denmark. Sørensen lives in Denmark on the island of Mors.

Michael Goldman taught himself Danish over 30 years ago to help him win the heart of a lovely Danish girl—and they have been married ever since. Over 90 of his translations have appeared in numerous journals including Rattle, The International Poetry Review, and World Literature Today. Also a carpenter and clarinetist, Goldman lives in Florence, Massachusetts, USA. www.hammerandhorn.net

www.ingramcontent.com/pod-product-compliance
Lightning Source LLC
Chambersburg PA
CBHW030108240426
43661CB00031B/1339/J